Fact Finders®

MILITARY HEROES

NAVAJO CODE TALKERS
SECRET AMERICAN INDIAN HEROES OF WORLD WAR II

BY BRYNN BAKER

CAPSTONE PRESS
a capstone imprint

Fact Finders Books are published by Capstone Press,
1710 Roe Crest Drive, North Mankato, Minnesota 56003
www.capstonepub.com

Copyright © 2016 by Capstone Press, a Capstone imprint. All rights reserved. No part of this publication may be reproduced in whole or in part, or stored in a retrieval system, or transmitted in any form or by any means, electronic, mechanical, photocopying, recording, or otherwise, without written permission of the publisher.

Library of Congress Cataloging-in-Publication Data
Baker, Brynn.
  Navajo code talkers : secret American Indian Heroes of World War II / by Brynn Baker.
    pages cm.—(Fact finders. Military heroes)
  Includes bibliographical references and index.
  Summary: "Discusses the heroic actions and experiences of the Navajo code talkers and the impact they made during times of war and conflict"—Provided by publisher.
  Audience: Ages 8-10.
  ISBN 978-1-4914-4837-3 (library binding)
  ISBN 978-1-4914-4905-9 (paperback)
  ISBN 978-1-4914-4923-3 (eBook PDF)
1. World War, 1939–1945—Cryptography—Juvenile literature. 2. World War, 1939–1945—Participation, Indian—Juvenile literature. 3. Navajo language—Juvenile literature. 4. Navajo code talkers—Juvenile literature. 5. Navajo Indians—History—20th century—Juvenile literature. 6. United States. Marine Corps—Indian troops--Juvenile literature. I. Title.

D810.C88B33 2016
940.54'8673—dc23

2015017098

Editorial Credits
Editor: Jennifer Loomis
Designer: Veronica Scott
Media Researcher: Eric Gohl
Production Specialist: Tori Abraham

Photo Credits
AP Photo: Felicia Fonseca, 29; Capstone: 13; Corbis: Underwood & Underwood, 4; CriaImages.com: Jay Robert Nash Collection, 5, 11, 14; Library of Congress: 8, 10, 12, 18, 21; National Archives and Records Administration: 9; Newscom: UPI Photo Service/Michael Kleinfeld, 27, ZUMA Press/Greg Sorber, 17; United States Marine Corps History Division: cover, 7, 19, 22, 23, 25
Design Elements: Shutterstock

Primary Source Bibliography
Page 16—Tom Gorman. "Navajos Honored for War of Words." *Los Angeles Times*, 26 July 2001.
Page 24—"Semper Fidelis, Code Talkers." http://www.archives.gov/publications/prologue/2001/winter/navajo-code-talkers.html. Retrieved June 2, 2015.
Page 24—"Navajo Code Talkers and the Unbreakable Code." https://www.cia.gov/news-information featured-story-archive/2008-featured-story-archive/navajo-code-talkers/. Retrieved June 2, 2015.
Page 27—"Remarks by the President in a Ceremony Honoring the Navajo Code Talkers." http://georgewbush-whitehouse.archives.gov/news/releases/2001/07/20010726-5.html. Retrieved June 2, 2015.
Page 29—"Decoding history: A World War II Navajo Code Talker in his own words." http://inamerica blogs.cnn.com/2011/12/04/decoding-history-a-world-war-ii-navajo-code-talker-in-his-own-words/. Retrieved June 2, 2015.

TABLE OF CONTENTS

Chapter 1
America Joins World War II 4

Chapter 2
Navajo Indians 10

Chapter 3
Creating the Code 16

Chapter 4
Navajo Code Talkers 22

TIMELINE 28
CRITICAL THINKING USING THE COMMON CORE 29
GLOSSARY 30
READ MORE 31
INTERNET SITES 31
INDEX 32

CHAPTER 1

AMERICA JOINS WORLD WAR II

World War II (1939–1945) was a global war. It involved most of the world's nations. Powerful countries formed military **alliances**. These alliances involved more than 100 million people from 30 different countries. It quickly became the most widespread war in history.

In 1937 Japan was at war with China and controlled most of Asia. The United States stopped exporting steel, iron, and **aviation** fuel to Japan. This was done to weaken Japan's ability to attack nations in the Pacific.

Soldiers working for the Japanese Army's Radio Corps were specially trained to use radio equipment during World War II.

alliance—an agreement between groups to work together
aviation—the science of building and flying aircraft

Japan's attack on Pearl Harbor lasted two hours. The Japanese destroyed about 20 American ships, including eight huge battleships and nearly 200 airplanes.

Even so, the Japanese unexpectedly attacked the U.S. Navy at Pearl Harbor in Hawaii. The Japanese had listened to American radio broadcasts. They knew the U.S. naval fleet was stationed at Pearl Harbor. On December 7, 1941, Japanese fighter jets dropped bombs on American soldiers who were still asleep in their beds. More than 2,400 civilians and American soldiers died in the attack.

President Franklin D. Roosevelt quickly declared war on Japan. Within two weeks he demanded an air attack on Japan's mainland. American planes, ships, and troops were spread out across entire oceans and in many different countries. Victory depended on the U.S. military finding ways to communicate. They needed to share locations and battle plans without their enemies using the information against them.

Fun Fact:

In the 1940s the U.S. military developed wireless radios to send and receive messages.

Philip Johnston's Idea

The U.S. military created secret codes for their messages. However, the Japanese were quick to **decipher** them. So the Americans made the codes more difficult. But then the codes became so complicated that it took hours to translate simple messages. During combat delayed messages could be deadly. They needed a simple, yet unbreakable, code.

Philip Johnston, an engineer from Los Angeles, read about the military's efforts to create such a code. He believed he had the solution. As the son of **missionaries**, Johnston grew up on a Navajo Indian reservation. He knew that a code based on the Navajo language would be nearly impossible to break.

Speaking Navajo

In Navajo each syllable carries meaning and must be spoken perfectly. The slightest mistake in pronunciation or **tone** can change the entire meaning of a word. This makes Navajo one of the hardest languages to understand and speak. The Navajo language even confuses other American Indian tribes.

Philip Johnston

In 1896 when Philip Johnston was 4 years old, his missionary family moved to Arizona to work on a Navajo reservation. Johnston grew up with Navajo children. He played with them and learned the Navajo language and customs. When he was 9 years old, Johnston served as interpreter at a conference between Navajo leaders and President Theodore Roosevelt.

decipher—to figure out something that is written in code or is hard to understand
missionary—a person who does religious or charitable work in a territory or foreign country
tone—a way of speaking or writing that shows a certain feeling or attitude

Johnston contacted Marine Corps offices and set up a meeting with Major James E. Jones. He convinced Jones that the difficulty of the Navajo language combined with a secret code would be impossible to break. The Japanese would no longer be able to understand U.S. radio communications.

In March 1942 Jones arranged for Johnston to meet with Major General Clayton Vogel and Colonel Wethered Woodward from the U.S. Marines. The meeting went well. The Marines agreed to try Johnston's idea. Now they needed to find Navajos willing to **enlist** in the Marines.

Navajo homes are called hogans. They are made from wooden poles, tree bark, and mud. Hogans are similar to log cabins except they are round. The doors to hogans are always located on the east side so the sun can enter the homes in the morning. Each hogan has one room with a dirt floor. Many Navajo families have more than one hogan.

```
                                    HEADQUARTERS,
                            AMPHIBIOUS FORCE, PACIFIC FLEET,
15/11-jwa                    CAMP ELLIOTT, SAN DIEGO, CALIFORNIA
                                                        March 6, 1942

        From:       The Commanding General.
        To:         The Commandant, U. S. Marine Corps.

        Subject:    Enlistment of Navaho Indians.

        Enclosures: (A) Brochure by Mr. Philip Johnston, with maps.
                    (B) Messages used in demonstration.

              1.    Mr. Philip Johnston of Los Angeles recently
        offered his services to this force to demonstrate the use of
        Indians for the transmission of messages by telephone and
        voice-radio. His offer was accepted and the demonstration
        was held for the Commanding General and his staff.

              2.    The demonstration was interesting and success-
        ful. Messages were transmitted and received almost verbatim.
        In conducting the demonstration messages were written by a
        member of the staff and handed to the Indian; he would trans-
        mit the message in his tribal dialect and the Indian on the
        other end would write them down in English. The text of
        messages as written and received are enclosed. The Indians
        do not have many military terms in their dialect so it was
        necessary to give them a few minutes, before the demonstra-
        tion, to improvise words for dive-bombing, anti-tank gun, etc.

              3.    Mr. Johnston stated that the Navaho is the only
        tribe in the United States that has not been infested with
        German students during the past twenty years. These Germans,
        studying the various tribal dialects under the guise of art
        students, anthropologists, etc., have undoubtedly attained a
        good working knowledge of all tribal dialects except Navaho.
        For this reason the Navaho is the only tribe available offer-
        ing complete security for the type of work under consideration.
        It is noted in Mr. Johnston's article (enclosed) that the Nav-
        aho is the largest tribe but the lowest in literacy. He stat-
        ed, however, that 1,000 — if that many were needed — could
        be found with the necessary qualifications. It should also be
        noted that the Navaho tribal dialect is completely unintellig-
        ible to all other tribes and all other people, with the poss-
        ible exception of as many as 28 Americans who have made a study
        of the dialect. This dialect is thus equivalent to a secret
        code to the enemy, and admirably suited for rapid, secure com-
        munication.
```

General Vogel's letter to the U.S. Marine Corps recommended finding 200 Navajo Indians to join the Marines and help with the secret code project.

enlist— to voluntarily join a branch of the military

CHAPTER 2

Navajo Indians

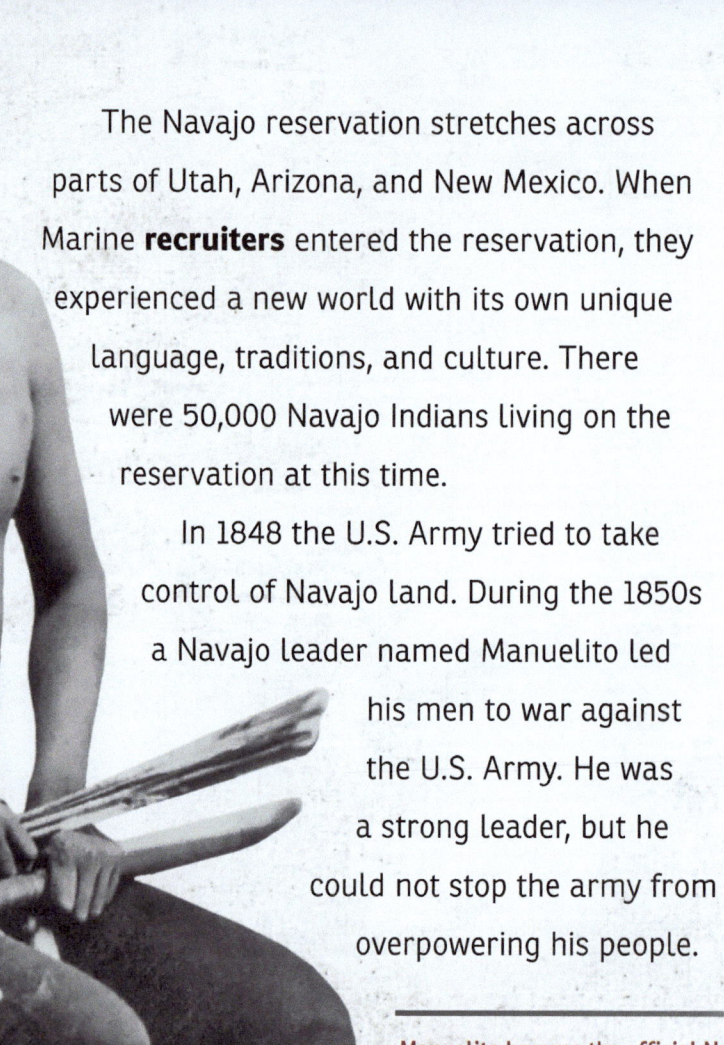

The Navajo reservation stretches across parts of Utah, Arizona, and New Mexico. When Marine **recruiters** entered the reservation, they experienced a new world with its own unique language, traditions, and culture. There were 50,000 Navajo Indians living on the reservation at this time.

In 1848 the U.S. Army tried to take control of Navajo land. During the 1850s a Navajo leader named Manuelito led his men to war against the U.S. Army. He was a strong leader, but he could not stop the army from overpowering his people.

Manuelito became the official Navajo chief in 1855. He was one of 25 leaders who signed the Navajo Treaty of 1868, which allowed the Navajo Indians to return to their homeland.

In 1864 more than 8,500 Navajo Indians were captured in Arizona. They were forced to walk 300 miles (483 kilometers) to Fort Sumner in New Mexico. Navajo people called this forced walk the Long Walk. Many did not survive the journey. Those who did found themselves held **captive** in a strange land.

> Navajo Indians lived under armed guard at Fort Sumner. Many tried to escape the terrible conditions. The land was not good for farming, and there was a lack of clean water to drink. The only shelter some Navajo people had were holes they dug in the ground. The openings were covered with animal hides or branches for protection against the cold of winter and the heat of summer. More than 3,000 Navajo Indians died while being held captive at Fort Sumner.

recruiter—a person who signs up new members of the military force
captive—confined to a place and not able to escape

Four years later the U.S. government allowed the Navajo Indians to return to their homeland. However, it had been turned into a reservation. There, Navajos were forced to adopt American customs. Navajo children got into trouble at school if they spoke their native language instead of English.

The Navajo Treaty of 1868 promised a free education to Navajo children. The purpose of this education was to rid Navajo Indians of their culture and force them to fit into white society. Many Navajo children were sent to government-run boarding schools far from their reservations. This long-distance separation was meant to speed up their adoption of white culture.

The Navajo reservation is located where Arizona, Utah, New Mexico, and Colorado meet. This is why the reservation's location is known as the Four Corners.

Did You Know?

The Navajo Indians have the largest reservation in the United States. The reservation covers 27,000 square miles (70,000 sq km) of land.

The U.S. government had treated the Navajo people unfairly for decades. However, this did not stop the government from asking Navajos for help during World War II. Marine recruiters were surprised to see the long line of Navajo volunteers willing to enlist in the U.S. military. At this point the code project was secret. The Navajo men had no idea what awaited them as Marines.

Boot Camp

The first task for any new Marine is to complete basic training, known as boot camp. In 1942, 29 Navajo recruits were sent to San Diego, California. It was the first time they had ever been on a bus. Many had never even left the reservation or seen city lights.

Like most Marines the Navajo men struggled to complete the seven weeks of training. However, they struggled for very different reasons. Most new recruits found it hard to complete the challenging physical fitness tests, but not the Navajo recruits.

Having long hair is a cultural tradition for Navajo people. Many Navajo Indians wear their hair long and loose or tied back in a traditional Navajo bun.

The Navajo Indians were used to hard work and exercise. They grew up living off the land—having to hunt, fish, haul water, and build homes. It was the seemingly smaller requirements of boot camp that were difficult for the Navajo recruits. In many ways military expectations were at odds with Navajo traditions and culture. Navajo Indians often wore their hair long. As Marines they had to wear their hair in short, military-style crew cuts. Navajos also believe eye contact is disrespectful. In the military it is a form of respect and discipline. Even wearing a uniform was uncomfortable for many of the Navajo men. However, all 29 Navajo recruits graduated from boot camp and went on to their next level of training.

Fun Fact:

The minimum age to enlist in the U.S. military is 18. However, some Navajo Indians lied about their age to be accepted. One recruit was only 15 years old when he enlisted.

CHAPTER 3
CREATING THE CODE

The Navajo recruits were sent to Camp Elliott in Southern California. There, they were finally told about the code project. The men were taught about basic electronics and how to communicate through radio broadcasts. They learned how to use, care for, and repair the radios that would eventually send their messages. But first they had to create the unbreakable code.

"The brass came by and told us to use our language to come up with words representing the letters A to Z, and to come up with a code for military terms," explained Navajo code talker Chester Nez. "They put us all in a room to work it out and, at first, everybody thought we'd never make it. It seemed impossible because even among ourselves, we didn't agree on all the right Navajo words." Despite the difficulty of this task, the men worked together and soon created the perfect code.

Chester Nez (front row, center) was only in 10th grade when he became one of the original 29 Navajo code talkers. Nez was the last of the original code talkers to pass away. He died on June 4, 2014, at the age of 93.

Navajo people value silence because it shows good listening skills. They are very comfortable with being silent around other people for long periods of time.

First they created a list of English words to stand for each letter of the alphabet (A=apple, B=bear, C=cat). Then they translated the English word to Navajo (apple=be-la-sana, bear=shush, cat=moasi). Next these Navajo code words were used to represent each letter of the alphabet (A=be-la-sana, B=shush, and C=moasi).

The Navajo men then took it a step further. They used three words to represent each English letter (A=apple, ant, ax). They used the three words **interchangeably** to make the code harder to **interpret**. The Navajo translation for the letter A was now coded as be-la-sana, wol-la-chee, or tse-nill. For example, to communicate the word "navy" over the radio, the men would say the Navajo code word for each letter—n, a, v, y (nesh-chee, wol-la-chee, a-keh-di-glini, tsah-as-zih).

Navajo code talkers Preston Toledo (left) and Frank Toledo (right) were cousins. Preston Toledo was only 18 when he joined the Marines. With his small size, he did not weigh enough to meet the Marine's requirements. To solve this problem, he drank a large amount of water before enlisting to add extra pounds to his weight.

interchangeable—easily switched with someone or something else
interpret—to decide what something means

Sample of the Navajo Dictionary

English Letter	Navajo Word	Meaning
A	Wol-la-chee	Ant
B	Shush	Bear
C	Ba-goshi	Cow
D	Lha-cha-eh	Dog
E	Dzeh	Elk
F	Ma-e	Fox
G	Ah-tad	Girl
H	Lin	Horse
I	Tkin	Ice
J	Yil-doi	Jerk
K	Klizzie-yazzie	Kid
L	Ah-jad	Leg
M	Na-as-tso-si	Mouse
N	A-chin	Nose
O	Ne-ahs-jah	Owl
P	Bi-so-dih	Pig
Q	Ca-yeilth	Quiver
R	Gah	Rabbit
S	Klesh	Snake
T	A-woh	Tooth
U	Shi-da	Uncle
V	A-keh-di-glini	Victor
W	Gloe-ih	Weasel
X	Al-an-as-dzoh	Cross
Y	Tsah-as-zih	Yucca
Z	Besh-do-gliz	Zinc

English Word	Navajo Word	Meaning
Corps	Din-neh-ih	Clan
Switchboard	Ya-ih-e-tih-ih	Central
Dive Bomber	Gini	Chicken Hawk
Torpedo plane	Tas-chizzie	Swallow
Observation plane	Ne-as-jah	Owl
Fighter plane	Da-he-tih-hi	Hummingbird
Bomber	Jay-sho	Buzzard
Alaska	Beh-hga	With-Winter
America	Ne-he-mah	Our Mother
Australia	Cha-yes-desi	Rolled Hat
Germany	Besh-be-cha-he	Iron Hat
Philippines	Ke-yah-da-na-lhe	Floating Land

Source: U.S. National Archives and Records Administration

Thankfully not all words had to be spelled out and coded letter-by-letter. The Navajo men compared the military to nature and chose words to represent common terms. Fighter planes flew quickly like hummingbirds, so they were given the Navajo code name da-he-tih-hi. Battleships were compared to whales and were coded lo-tso. Submarines were besh-lo, meaning "iron fish." The United States was coded ne-he-mah, which means "our mother."

The Navajo men practiced sending and translating the code over the radio. They trained until they could send and translate three-line messages in 20 seconds without any mistakes. The slightest error could change the entire meaning and put troops in danger.

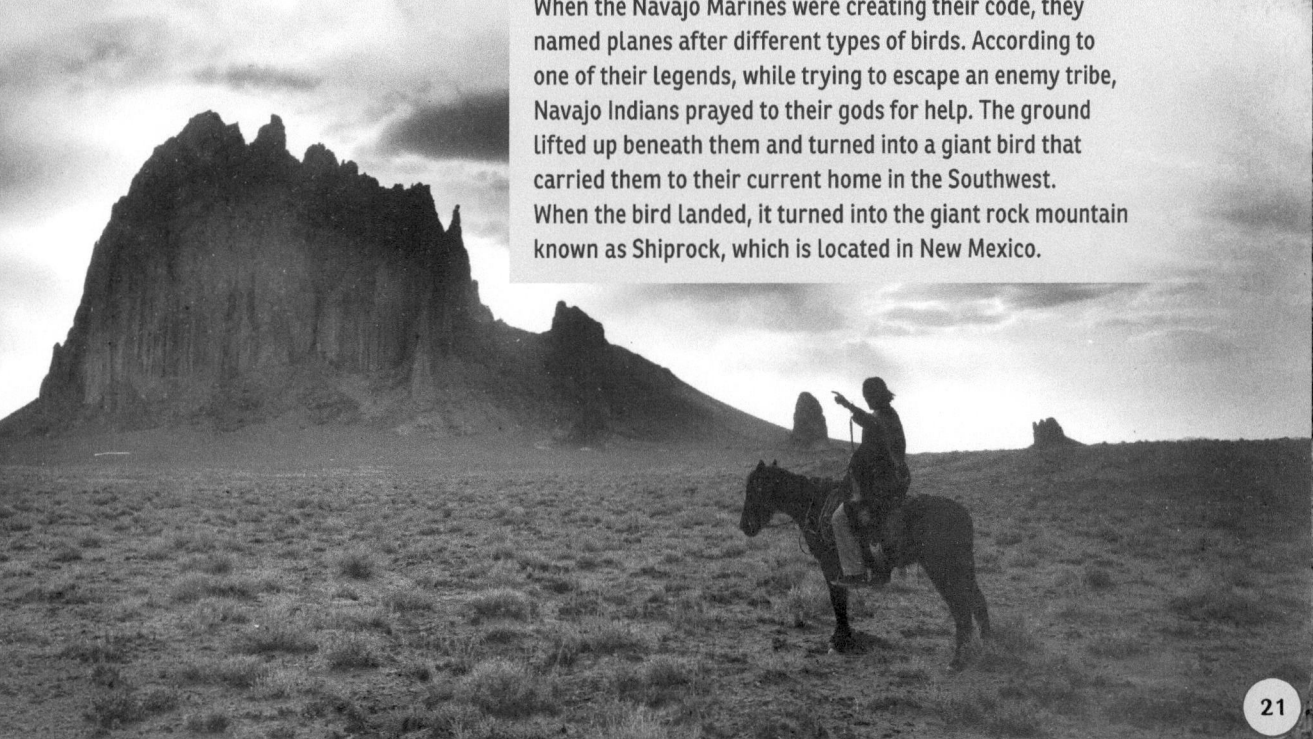

When the Navajo Marines were creating their code, they named planes after different types of birds. According to one of their legends, while trying to escape an enemy tribe, Navajo Indians prayed to their gods for help. The ground lifted up beneath them and turned into a giant bird that carried them to their current home in the Southwest. When the bird landed, it turned into the giant rock mountain known as Shiprock, which is located in New Mexico.

CHAPTER 4
Navajo Code Talkers

Marine Corps leaders were so impressed with the code that they made the program larger. Philip Johnston was put in charge of recruiting more Navajo Indians. Most came from the reservation. Some transferred from other branches of the military. The group quickly grew to include more than 400 men.

Two of the original 29 code talkers, Johnny Manuelito (top row, third from left) and John Benally (second row, fifth from lef earned very high marks during training and were asked to stay at Camp Elliott as teache It was their job to teach the code to new, incoming recruits.

The Japanese were very good at finding the location of radio signals. This meant the code talkers had to be skilled at setting up their equipment, sending and receiving codes, and then running away to a new location as quickly as possible.

Navajo code talkers were sent to war during the summer of 1942. They were often among the first wave of troops to **storm** enemy positions. They had to run while carrying their bulky radios. They also had to set up their equipment while under heavy enemy fire. Many dug trenches and worked in **foxholes** to protect themselves. The Navajo code talkers sent and translated messages to U.S. troops in most of the major battles in the Pacific. They reported locations, sent updates, and called in **reinforcements**.

Did You Know?

Out of 400 Navajo code talkers, 13 died in battle.

storm—to attack suddenly or violently
foxhole—a hole dug for a soldier to sit or lie in for protection from the enemy
reinforcements—extra troops sent into battle

Iwo Jima

Iwo Jima is an island belonging to Japan. It was the location of a key February–March 1945 battle during World War II. During the battle six code talkers worked day and night to send more than 800 messages without a single mistake. The code worked exactly as Philip Johnston and the Marines had hoped. U.S. troops received important messages, and enemy ears could not understand any of the radio broadcast. This helped the United States capture Iwo Jima and eventually win the war. The Navajo men were "the simplest, fastest, and most reliable" way to send secret messages, wrote Marine Captain Ralph Sturkey in his Iwo Jima battle report. The Japanese never broke the Navajo code and surrendered in August 1945.

"Were it not for the Navajo, the Marines would never have taken Iwo Jima."

—Marine Major Howard Connor

Carl Nelson Gorman was one of the original 29 code talkers. After the war he attended art school. He later became an instructor of Native American art and art history at the University of California, Davis. Gorman's artwork is shown in galleries around the world.

From Classified to Celebrated

The Navajo code talkers were not allowed to talk about their experience when they returned home. Their code was **classified**. The Marines wanted to keep it a secret in case they needed to use it again in future battles. Very few people knew about the Navajo code talkers and the role they played in winning World War II. Instead they quietly went back to their lives on the reservation.

In 1969 the military officially released the secret code. After that, the story of the Navajo code talkers spread across the country. In 1982 President Ronald Reagan declared August 14 National Navajo Code Talker Day. In April 2000 New Mexico Senator Jeff Bingaman proposed an act to honor the code talkers. The act's purpose was to recognize the code talkers' heroic actions during World War II. The unique service they provided to the United States saved countless lives and helped to end the war. Later that year President Bill Clinton signed the act into law.

classified—top secret

On July 26, 2001, President George W. Bush awarded the 29 original code talkers with Congressional Gold Medals. Only five were still alive to accept the award. Families of the other men accepted the medals on their behalf at the ceremony in Washington, D.C. The Navajo code talkers "brought honor to their nation and victory to their country," said President Bush. Silver medals were awarded to every Navajo code talker at a ceremony in Arizona later that year. "All Americans owe these men a debt of gratitude," said Senator Ben Nighthorse Campbell of Colorado. The Navajo code talkers had bravely served their country and were finally given their place in history.

Navajo code talker Allen Dale June (left) received a Congressional Gold Medal for his service in World War II. He enlisted in the Marines at the age of 16 by telling recruiters he was older. June served in the war from 1941 to 1945. He reached the rank of sergeant.

TIMELINE

1864
The U.S. Army defeats the Navajo Indians and forces many of them to walk 300 miles (483 km) to Fort Sumner in New Mexico.

1868
Navajos are allowed to move back to their homeland, which has become a reservation.

December 7, 1941
Japan attacks Pearl Harbor. The United States enters World War II one day later on December 8, 1941.

1942
Navajo code talkers begin training for and serving in World War II.

February–March 1945
Battle of Iwo Jima

August 14, 1945
Japan surrenders, bringing World War II to an end.

August 14, 1982
President Ronald Reagan declares August 14 National Navajo Code Talker Day.

December 21, 2000
President Bill Clinton signs into law an act that honors the code talkers.

2001
President George W. Bush presents Congressional Gold Medals to the 29 original code talkers. Silver medals are awarded to all code talkers.

CRITICAL THINKING USING THE COMMON CORE

1. Explain why the Navajo language was a good language to use as a code during World War II. Use details from the text to support your answer. (Key Ideas and Details)

2. Suppose that the Navajo Indians had refused to help the U.S. government create a code for World War II. How do you think this refusal would have affected the war? (Integration of Knowledge and Ideas)

3. The Navajo Indians agreed to help a government that treated them terribly. Why do you think they did this? (Text Type and Purposes)

"Our Navajo code was one of the most important military secrets of World War II. The fact that the Marines did not tell us Navajo men how to develop the code indicated their trust in us and in our abilities. The feeling that I could make it in both the white world and the Navajo world began there, and it has stayed with me all of my life. For that I am grateful."

—Navajo code talker Chester Nez

GLOSSARY

alliance (uh-LY-uhnts)—an agreement between groups to work together

aviation (ay-vee-AY-shuhn)—the science of building and flying aircraft

captive (KAP-tiv)—confined to a place and not able to escape

classified (KLAH-suh-fide)—top secret

decipher (di-SYE-fur)—to figure out something that is written in code or is hard to understand

enlist (en-LIST)—to voluntarily join a branch of the military

foxhole (FAHKS-hohl)—a hole dug for a soldier to sit or lie in for protection from the enemy

interchangeable (in-tur-CHAYN-juh-buhl)—easily switched with someone or something else

interpret (in-TUR-prit)—to decide what something means

missionary (MISH-uh-ner-ee)—a person who does religious or charitable work in a territory or foreign country

recruiter (ri-KROOT-uhr)—a person who signs up new members of the military force

reinforcements (ree-in-FORSS-muhnts)—extra troops sent into battle

storm (STORM)—to attack suddenly or violently

tone (TOHN)—a way of speaking or writing that shows a certain feeling or attitude

READ MORE

Barber, Nicola. *Who Broke the Wartime Codes?* Primary Source Detectives. Chicago: Heinemann Library, 2014.

Cunningham, Kevin, and Peter Benoit. *The Navajo. A True Book.* New York: Children's Press, 2011.

Gibson, Karen Bush. *Native American History for Kids: With 21 Activities.* Chicago: Chicago Review Press, 2010.

INTERNET SITES

FactHound offers a safe, fun way to find Internet sites related to this book. All of the sites on FactHound have been researched by our staff.

Here's all you do:
Visit **www.facthound.com**
Type in this code: 9781491448373

Check out projects, games and lots more at
www.capstonekids.com

INDEX

Benally, John, 22
Bingaman, Jeff, 26
boot camp, 14–15
Bush, George W., 27

Campbell, Ben Nighthorse, 27
Camp Elliott, 16, 22
Clinton, Bill, 26
Congressional Gold Medals, 27
Connor, Howard, 24

Fort Sumner, 11
Four Corners, 13

Gorman, Carl Nelson, 25

hogans, 8

Iwo Jima, 24

Japan, 4, 5, 6, 8, 23, 24
Johnston, Philip, 6, 7, 8, 22
Jones, James E., 8
June, Allen Dale, 27

Manuelito, Johnny, 22
Manuelito (Navajo leader), 10

National Navajo Code Talker Day, 26
Navajo code (creating), 16, 18–19, 21
Navajo dictionary, 20
Navajo Treaty of 1868, 10, 12
Nez, Chester, 16, 17, 29

Pearl Harbor, Hawaii, 5

Reagan, Ronald, 26
Roosevelt, Franklin D., 5

Shiprock, New Mexico, 21
Sturkey, Ralph, 24

Toledo, Frank, 19
Toledo, Preston, 19

Vogel, Clayton, 8, 9

wireless radios, 5, 19
Woodward, Wethered, 8
World War II, 4, 13, 24, 26, 27